DANIEL BOONE

by Tom Streissguth
illustrations by Loren Chantland

On My Own

BIOGRAPHY

Carolrhoda Books, Inc./Minneapolis

*To the frontier girls: Marie-Christine, Lou Lou,
and Adele — T. S.*

To my teacher Jack Mastrofski—I'm still learning, Jack —L. C.

The photograph on page 46 appears courtesy of the Massachusetts Historical Society.

Text copyright © 2002 by Tom Streissguth
Illustrations copyright © 2002 by Loren Chantland

This book is available in two editions:
Library binding by Carolrhoda Books, Inc., a division of Lerner Publishing Group
Soft cover by First Avenue Editions, an imprint of Lerner Publishing Group
241 First Avenue North
Minneapolis, MN 55401 U.S.A.

Website address: www.lernerbooks.com

Library of Congress Cataloging-in-Publication Data

Streissguth, Thomas, 1958–
    Daniel Boone / by Tom Streissguth ; illustrations by Loren Chantland.
    p. cm. — (On my own biography)
    ISBN 1-57505-520-1 (lib. bdg. : alk. paper)
    ISBN 1-57505-532-5 (pbk.)
    1. Boone, Daniel, 1734–1820—Juvenile literature. 2. Frontier and pioneer life—
Kentucky—Juvenile literature. 3. Pioneers—Kentucky—Biography—Juvenile
literature. 4. Kentucky—Biography—Juvenile literature. [1. Boone, Daniel,
1734–1820. 2. Pioneers. 3. Frontier and pioneer life.] I. Chantland, Loren, 1963– ill.
II. Title. III. Series.
F454.B66 S77 2002
976.9'02'092—dc21   00–011795

Manufactured in the United States of America
1 2 3 4 5 6 – JR – 07 06 05 04 03 02

Author's Note

When Daniel Boone was born in 1734, the United States of America did not yet exist. Since the late 1500s, Europeans had been settling small colonies in eastern North America. These settlers found that the land was already home to many other people, whom the Europeans called Indians. The new settlers, or colonists, began to buy or take the Indians' land, piece by piece.

While Daniel grew, the American colonies grew as well. As more settlers arrived and families added more children, they needed more land to farm. So they moved farther into the wilderness, into places where only Indians lived. These settlers faced hunger, wild animals, and attacks by Indians who wanted to protect their homes. One of the first and most famous of these American pioneers was Daniel Boone. This is his story.

Exeter, Pennsylvania
about 1740

Young Daniel Boone
could not stand to stay inside.
He loved to roam and play
in the woods near his home.
Daniel followed the sounds of calling birds.
He searched the ground for deer tracks
and tried to walk without making a sound.

When Daniel was about six years old,

smallpox came to Exeter.

This disease killed many people.

To keep their children safe,

Sarah and Squire Boone

told them to stay indoors.

Daniel hated being cooped up.

But he had an idea.

If he caught smallpox,

his parents might set him free.

One night, Daniel and his sister Elizabeth

slipped quietly outside.

They crept into a neighbor's house.

Then they crawled into bed

with friends who had smallpox.

Days later, Daniel grew sick and weak.

But he did not die.

Before long, he was exploring the woods again.

Daniel grew up strong.
He could walk for days
and chop wood for hours.

In the woods, Daniel met many hunters.

He sat by their warm campfires.

The hunters shared their food

and told stories about the wilderness.

Daniel met many Indians, too.
The Shawnee, the Delaware, and other tribes
were already living in Pennsylvania
when white settlers came.
Many American colonists
did not want the Indians around.

They wanted the land for themselves.
But Daniel eagerly learned
from Indian hunters.
Many times he wandered
with them through the woods.
He learned some of their words
and wore his hair like an Indian man.

Daniel's friends taught
him many things.
He learned how to set traps
and how to handle a long gun.

He learned to track
bear and deer
as well as a Shawnee hunter.

Daniel felt happiest when he was alone,
exploring a deep forest.
He ate nuts and berries.
He skinned and cooked
the animals he hunted.
Daniel Boone grew into a young man
who could find his own way
over mountains and through valleys.
He could cross rivers and streams,
follow winding trails,
and never get lost.

Wild Country

1750

When Daniel was 15 years old,
the Boones left Exeter.
Like many families,
the Boones wanted to settle new land.
They wanted to find their own place
in the growing American colonies.
The journey would be long and hard.

But Daniel knew the trails and
the woods better than anyone.
His family trusted him to guide them south.
The Boones headed to the Yadkin River Valley
in North Carolina.
This wild country had few settlers
and no towns.
Squire Boone had heard there was
good land everywhere,
waiting for the farmer's plow.

After the long journey, the Boones
reached the Yadkin River Valley.
Daniel helped Squire Boone clear the land.
Father and son moved big stones.
They dug tree stumps out of the earth.
Then they planted corn and wheat.
The work left Daniel tired and bored.
Each fall, after the harvest,
he eagerly took up his long gun.

He spent weeks hunting for food
to see his family through the cold winter.
He gathered skins and pelts to sell, too.
Daniel always took careful aim
with his long gun.
He had sharp eyes and steady hands.
In one good season, he killed 99 bears.

In 1753, Daniel met a young neighbor

named Rebecca Bryan.

Daniel liked the way

she looked straight at him.

She didn't mind his wandering.

And she could be stubborn, just like him.

Three years later,

Daniel and Rebecca married.

They moved to a farm of their own.

In 1757, Rebecca had a son named James.

Over the years,

 she had nine more children.

When James was big enough,

Daniel brought him hunting in the mountains.

At night, they lay near a blazing fire.

To keep his son warm,

Daniel tucked James into his deerskin coat.

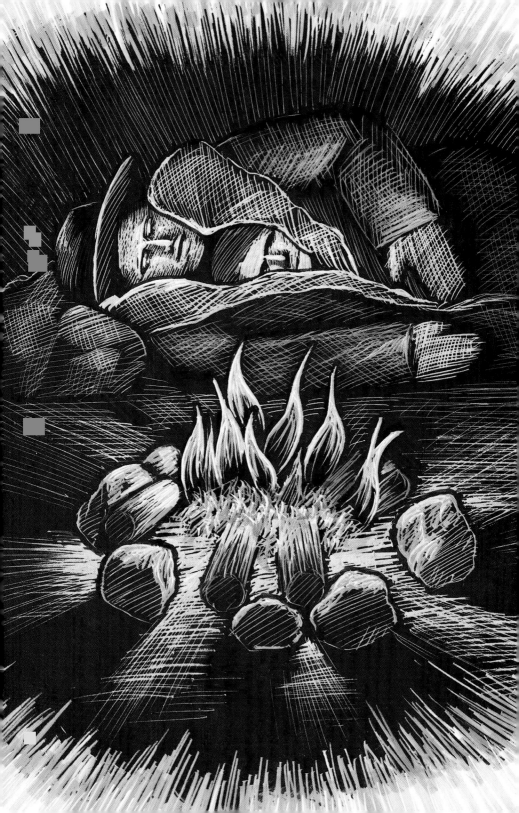

Many other families followed the Boones
to the Yadkin River Valley.
Game animals were becoming harder to find.
Daniel heard stories about land to the west,
across the Appalachian Mountains.
An old friend, John Findley,
told him all about Kentucky.
In this country, Findley said,
buffalo, elk, deer, and black bear roamed.

Beautiful meadows and clear streams
lay between the wooded hills.

Daniel listened closely.

In Kentucky, he could wander again.

He could help settle the country.

He would be the head of his clan,
like Squire Boone.

Daniel made up his mind.

He would go west, into the mountains
and toward the open country beyond.

Into Kentucky

In 1769, Daniel Boone and five other men

crossed the mountains

through the Cumberland Gap.

The land was as good

as John Findley had said.

For months, the men hunted and trapped.

But they were not alone.

Shawnee Indians already lived here.

One day, a group of Shawnee men

rushed into Daniel's camp.

They took the white men's pelts and horses.

The Shawnee leader, Captain Will,

gave an angry warning.

The white hunters must leave Kentucky

and never come back.

Daniel and John Stewart followed the Shawnee.

They stole back their horses.

But the Shawnee captured the two men.

After seven days, Daniel and John escaped.

The Shawnee did not chase them.

The raid frightened Daniel's friends.

Some went back east.

But Daniel would not give up his dream.

He spent more than a year in Kentucky,

scouting, hunting, and trapping.

For months at a time, he traveled alone.

He lived in caves in hillsides.

He built lean-tos by riverbanks.

To keep himself company,

he talked and sang out loud.

Daniel learned all he could about the land.

When the time was right for settling here,

he would be ready.

Finally, in the spring of 1771,
Daniel returned home.
He arrived at night.
He found Rebecca at a party,
laughing and dancing.

Daniel approached his wife
and asked her to dance.
She turned away
from the dirty, long-haired stranger.
Then she recognized the calm and friendly
voice of her missing husband.

Daniel settled down with his family again.

But he did not forget

the wild country of Kentucky.

Two years later, he led a group of families

hoping to build homes there.

Rebecca and the Boone children

were part of the group.

The settlers brought food, clothing, guns,

tools, horses, and a few cattle.

The youngest children rode in baskets

set on the horses' backs.

Daniel led the way along narrow trails
toward the Cumberland Gap.
The travelers had to be careful.
They were moving through hunting grounds
of the Shawnee and Cherokee Indians.

Daniel realized that the journey would be
harder than he had expected.

He sent a group back for more food.

Daniel's son James was among them.

The next day,

Daniel heard terrible news.

Indians had attacked James's camp.
Daniel sent his brother Squire
to find James.
Daniel stayed to defend the travelers
in case another attack came.
When Squire returned,
he told Daniel that James was dead.
So were most of the others.
Squire had found their bodies and buried them.

The settlers were scared.

The Indians were fighting to protect their land.

Kentucky seemed too dangerous.

Most of the settlers turned back.

But the Boones stayed near Kentucky
for the winter.

The next spring,
Daniel visited his son's lonely grave.

He covered the grave to protect it
from digging wolves.

A sudden storm broke
from a gray and gloomy sky.

Daniel sat quietly by the grave
and began to cry.

The Wilderness Road

Daniel Boone had lost his son in Kentucky.
But he still longed to live
on that beautiful, green land.
A man named Richard Henderson
gave Daniel a chance to return.
Henderson wanted to blaze a road
and build a town in the Kentucky wilderness.
He wanted Daniel to help him convince
the Cherokee Indians to give up the land.
And he wanted Daniel to lead
the building of the road.
In return, Daniel would earn
2,000 acres of land.

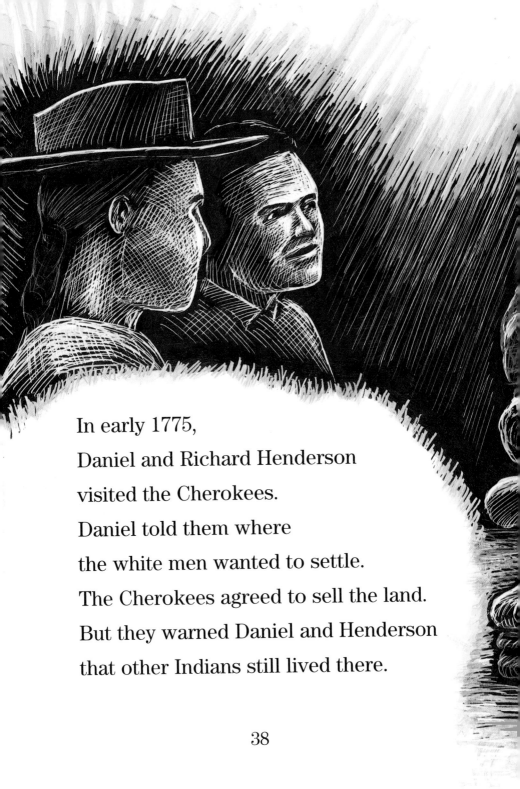

In early 1775,
Daniel and Richard Henderson
visited the Cherokees.
Daniel told them where
the white men wanted to settle.
The Cherokees agreed to sell the land.
But they warned Daniel and Henderson
that other Indians still lived there.

In March, Daniel gathered about 50 men
in northern Tennessee.
Together, they would build
the Wilderness Road.
They started out along an Indian trail
called the Warrior's Path.
The men cut down trees
and hacked through thick brush.

They built log bridges
over swamps and creeks.
When the weather turned rainy,
they struggled through mud.
When the weather turned cold,
they slipped in icy puddles.

After two weeks of work,

the men had almost reached Kentucky.

But then Indians attacked the road builders.

They killed two men and hurt another.

Several of the men turned back.

Daniel kept going.

He would settle here or die trying.

The men reached the Kentucky River in April.
Daniel chose a place for the new town.
The fast-flowing river would help
protect the area from attacks.
The men began building log houses.
They named the place Boonesborough,
after the man who had led them there.

That summer, Daniel Boone
returned to his family.
The Boones packed their things—
furniture, food, clothing, and animals.
They followed the Wilderness Road
that Daniel had blazed into Kentucky.
On September 8, 1775, Daniel and Rebecca
reached their new home.
And they began to build a new life
in Boonesborough.

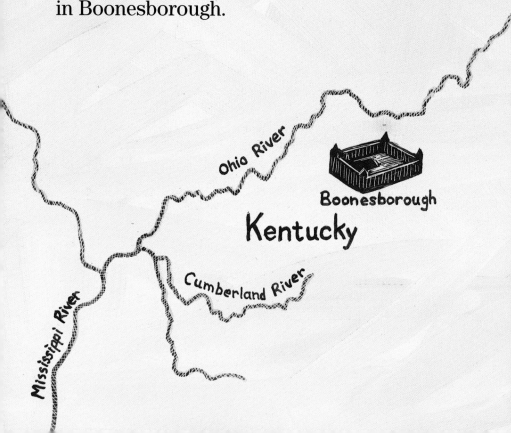

Ohio River

Boonesborough

Kentucky

Cumberland River

Mississippi River

Chester Harding, *Daniel Boone*, 1820

Afterword

For the next three years, Daniel Boone led the people of Boonesborough through hunger and danger. The town survived, and over time the Wilderness Road served as a path west for thousands of settlers. In 1783, the American colonies won independence from Great Britain. But Daniel never received the 2,000 acres he had earned for blazing the Wilderness Road and settling Boonesborough. The founders of the new nation, the United States of America, did not recognize Richard Henderson's claim to the land.

Daniel moved many more times and had many more adventures. Stories of his brave deeds spread all over the country. He had more conflicts with Indians who lived on the lands he hoped to settle. But unlike many settlers, Daniel never came to hate or fear the Indians. He formed friendships with some that lasted into his old age.

After he died in 1820, Daniel Boone became even more famous. For the people settling the American West, this heroic pioneer stood for open spaces and new opportunities. His courage, his skill as a hunter and trailblazer, and his respect for Indians have never been forgotten. His love for exploring and building homes on the frontier helped the United States of America grow into a great nation.

Important Dates

1734—Daniel Boone was born on October 22 in the
township of Exeter in the British colony of
Pennsylvania.

1750—Left Pennsylvania for North Carolina; went on
first long hunting trip

1756—Married Rebecca Bryan

1757—Birth of son, James, the first of 10 children

1769—Visited Kentucky; captured by Shawnee Indians;
escaped

1773—Led unsuccessful attempt to settle Kentucky;
son James killed in Indian attack

1775—Led blazing of Wilderness Road; founded
Boonesborough; brought family to Kentucky

1778—Captured by Shawnee Indians; lived with them
for months; escaped; defended Boonesborough
from Shawnee attack

1784—Publication of *The Adventures of Col. Daniel
Boon*, the first book about Boone. (His name
was misspelled in some early works.)

1799—Led family and other settlers into Missouri

1820—Died on September 26 in Missouri

48